NO-BAKE
DESSERTS

D1457031

Publications International, Ltd.

Pictured on the front cover *(clockwise from top left):* Chocolate Cookie Parfaits *(page 94),* Rocky Road Pudding *(page 46),* Cherry Parfait Crunch *(page 82)* and Easy Citrus Berry Shortcake *(page 106).*

Pictured on the back cover *(top to bottom):* No-Bake Bon Bon Cookies *(page 22),* Pistachio Ice Cream Pie *(page 24)* and Cinnamon-Honey Pops *(page 72).*

ISBN: 978-1-4508-9963-5

Library of Congress Control Number: 2014957812

Manufactured in China.

8 7 6 5 4 3 2 1

Microwave Cooking: Microwave ovens vary in wattage. Use the cooking times as guidelines and check for doneness before adding more time.

Preparation/Cooking Times: Preparation times are based on the approximate amount of time required to assemble the recipe before cooking, baking, chilling or serving. These times include preparation steps such as measuring, chopping and mixing. The fact that some preparations and cooking can be done simultaneously is taken into account. Preparation of optional ingredients and serving suggestions is not included.

Publications International, Ltd.

Contents

NO-BAKE BITES

Rocky Road Bundles

1 cup semisweet chocolate chips

½ cup creamy peanut butter

1 package (3 ounces) ramen noodles, any flavor, broken into bite-size pieces*

1 cup mini marshmallows

*Discard seasoning packet.

1. Line cookie sheet with waxed paper.

2. Combine chocolate chips and peanut butter in microwavable bowl. Microwave on MEDIUM (50%) 1 minute; stir. If necessary, repeat at additional 15-second intervals until chocolate is melted and mixture is smooth.

3. Add noodles and marshmallows; stir until well blended. Drop by tablespoonfuls onto prepared cookie sheet; refrigerate 1 hour or until firm.

MAKES 1 DOZEN TREATS

Cherry Cheesecake Squares

2 cups graham cracker crumbs

½ cup (1 stick) butter, melted

2 cups milk

1 package (4-serving size) cheesecake-flavored instant pudding and pie filling mix

4 cups frozen whipped topping, divided

1 can (21 ounces) cherry pie filling

1. Combine graham cracker crumbs and butter in medium bowl. Press into bottom of 13×9-inch baking pan.

2. Whisk milk into pudding mix in medium bowl until well blended. Fold in 2 cups whipped topping. Spread over crust. Spread pie filling evenly over pudding mixture. Spoon remaining 2 cups whipped topping over pie filling.

3. Refrigerate 2 hours or until chilled. Cut into squares.

MAKES 12 TO 16 SERVINGS

Easy Cocoa Oatmeal Cookies

1 cup sugar

1 cup flaked coconut

½ cup unsweetened cocoa powder

½ cup creamy peanut butter

½ cup milk

½ teaspoon vanilla

2 cups old-fashioned oats

1. Line cookie sheets with parchment paper.

2. Combine sugar, coconut, cocoa, peanut butter, milk and vanilla in medium saucepan; bring to a boil over medium-high heat. Add oats; stir until well blended. Remove from heat.

3. Drop dough by tablespoonfuls onto prepared baking sheets. Freeze 1 to 2 hours. Store in refrigerator.

MAKES 2 DOZEN COOKIES

Cherry Cheesecake Squares

No-Bake Gingersnap Balls

20 gingersnap cookies
(about 5 ounces)

⅓ cup powdered sugar

3 tablespoons dark
corn syrup

2 tablespoons creamy
peanut butter

1. Place cookies in large resealable food storage bag; crush finely with rolling pin or meat mallet. Place powdered sugar in shallow dish.

2. Combine corn syrup and peanut butter in medium bowl. Add crushed gingersnaps; stir until well blended. (Mixture should hold together without being sticky. If mixture is too dry, stir in additional 1 tablespoon corn syrup.)

3. Shape mixture into 24 (1-inch) balls; roll in powdered sugar to coat.

MAKES 2 DOZEN COOKIES

Tip: Some gingersnaps are crisper than others, so you might need to add an additional 1 to 2 tablespoons corn syrup to the crumb mixture in order for it to hold together.

Banana Pudding Squares

1 cup graham cracker crumbs

2 tablespoons butter, melted

1 package (8 ounces) cream cheese, softened

3 cups milk

2 packages (4-serving size) banana cream instant pudding and pie filling mix

1 container (8 ounces) whipped topping, divided

2 medium bananas

1. Line 13×9-inch baking pan with foil; spray with nonstick cooking spray.

2. Combine graham cracker crumbs and butter in small bowl; stir until well blended. Press into bottom of prepared pan.

3. Beat cream cheese in large bowl with electric mixer at low speed until smooth. Add milk and pudding mix; beat at high speed 2 minutes or until smooth and creamy. Fold in half of whipped topping until well blended. Reserve half of pudding mixture; spread remaining pudding mixture over crust.

4. Peel bananas; cut into ¼-inch slices. Arrange bananas evenly over pudding layer. Spoon reserved pudding mixture over bananas. Spread remaining whipped topping evenly over pudding mixture.

5. Cover loosely with plastic wrap and refrigerate 2 hours or up to 8 hours.

MAKES 18 SERVINGS

Chocolate & Peanut Butter Truffles

¾ cup (1½ sticks) butter (no substitutes)

1 cup REESE'S Peanut Butter Chips

½ cup HERSHEY'S Cocoa

1 can (14 ounces) sweetened condensed milk (not evaporated milk)

1 tablespoon vanilla extract

HERSHEY'S Cocoa or finely chopped nuts or graham cracker crumbs

1. Melt butter and peanut butter chips in saucepan over very low heat. Add cocoa; stir until smooth. Add sweetened condensed milk; stir constantly until mixture is thick and glossy, about 4 minutes. Remove from heat; stir in vanilla.

2. Refrigerate 2 hours or until firm enough to handle. Shape into 1-inch balls; roll in cocoa, nuts or graham cracker crumbs. Refrigerate until firm, about 1 hour. Store, covered, in refrigerator.

MAKES ABOUT 3½ DOZEN CANDIES

Prep Time: 30 minutes
Cook Time: 7 minutes
Chill Time: 3 hours

Cranberry Chocolate Chip Cereal Squares

6½ cups corn or rice cereal squares, divided

1 package (6 ounces) dried cranberries (about 1⅓ cups)

½ cup (1 stick) butter

1 package (about 10 ounces) mini marshmallows

1 cup semisweet chocolate chips

1. Line 13×9-inch baking pan with foil, leaving 2-inch overhang on two sides. Spray with nonstick cooking spray.

2. Coarsely crush 2 cups cereal in large bowl with back of spoon or hands. Stir in cranberries.

3. Melt butter in large saucepan overlow heat. Add marshmallows; stir constantly until marshmallows are melted and mixture is smooth. Remove from heat; stir in remaining 4½ cups whole cereal and crushed cereal mixture until well blended. Stir in chocolate chips. Press mixture into prepared pan.

4. Cover and refrigerate 30 minutes or until firm. Remove from pan using foil; cut into squares.

MAKES ABOUT 2½ DOZEN SQUARES

Crispy Cupcakes

¼ cup (½ stick) plus 2 tablespoons butter, divided

1 package (10½ ounces) marshmallows

½ cup creamy peanut butter

6 cups crisp rice cereal

1 cup bittersweet or semisweet chocolate chips

1½ cups powdered sugar

¼ cup milk

1. Spray 13×9-inch baking pan with nonstick cooking spray. Microwave 2 tablespoons butter in large microwavable bowl on HIGH 30 seconds or until melted. Add marshmallows; stir until coated with butter. Microwave on HIGH 1 minute; stir. Microwave 45 seconds; stir until melted. Add peanut butter; stir until well blended. Add cereal; stir until blended.

2. Spread mixture in prepared pan, using waxed paper to spread and press into even layer. Let stand 10 to 15 minutes or until set.

3. Meanwhile, place remaining ¼ cup butter and chocolate chips in medium microwavable bowl. Microwave on HIGH 40 seconds; stir. Microwave at additional 15-second intervals until melted and smooth. Gradually beat in powdered sugar and milk until well blended. Refrigerate until ready to use.

4. Spray 1½-inch round cookie or biscuit cutter with nonstick cooking spray; cut out 36 circles from cereal bars. Place small dab of frosting on top of 18 circles; top with remaining 18 circles, pressing down firmly to seal. Place "cupcakes" in paper baking cups, if desired. Pipe or spread frosting on cupcakes.

MAKES 1½ DOZEN CUPCAKES

Trail Mix Truffles

⅓ cup dried apples

¼ cup dried apricots

¼ cup apple butter

2 tablespoons golden raisins

1 tablespoon peanut butter

½ cup granola

¼ cup graham cracker crumbs, divided

¼ cup mini chocolate chips

1 tablespoon water

1. Combine apples, apricots, apple butter, raisins and peanut butter in food processor or blender; process until smooth. Stir in granola, 1 tablespoon graham cracker crumbs, chocolate chips and water. Shape mixture into 16 balls.

2. Place remaining graham cracker crumbs in shallow dish; roll balls in crumbs to coat. Cover and refrigerate until ready to serve.

MAKES 16 TRUFFLES

No-Bake Noodle Cookies

2 cups crisp chow mein noodles

⅔ cup semisweet chocolate chips

½ cup peanut butter chips

½ cup cocktail peanuts

⅓ cup raisins

1. Line cookie sheets with waxed paper or parchment paper.

2. Place noodles, chocolate chips, peanut butter chips, peanuts and raisins in large microwavable bowl. Microwave on HIGH 1 minute; stir. If necessary, microwave at additional 15-second intervals until chocolate is melted. Stir until well blended.

3. Drop noodle mixture by teaspoonfuls onto prepared cookie sheets. Refrigerate 1 hour. Store cookies between sheets of waxed paper in airtight container in refrigerator.

MAKES 2 DOZEN COOKIES

Trail Mix Truffles

Cheesecake Bites with Ginger-Berry Topping

8 gingersnap cookies (2-inch diameter)

4 ounces cream cheese, softened

1 package (4-serving size) cheesecake-flavored instant pudding and pie filling mix

1¼ cups milk

GINGER-BERRY TOPPING

½ cup blueberry preserves

¾ cup fresh or thawed frozen blueberries

1 teaspoon ground ginger

1. Line 24 mini (1¾-inch) muffin cups with paper baking cups. Break gingersnaps into pieces; process in food processor to make about ½ cup fine crumbs. Place 1 teaspoon crumbs in each cup.

2. Beat cream cheese in medium bowl with electric mixer at low speed until smooth. Add pudding mix and milk; beat at high speed 2 minutes or until creamy. Spoon rounded tablespoon cream cheese mixture into each cup. Place pan in freezer while preparing topping.

3. Place preserves in medium microwavable bowl; microwave on HIGH 15 seconds. Stir in blueberries and ginger.

4. Remove pan from freezer. Spoon 1 teaspoon topping over cream cheese layer in each cup. Serve immediately or cover with plastic wrap and refrigerate until ready to serve (up to 2 hours).

MAKES 2 DOZEN CHEESECAKE BITES

No-Bake Bon Bon Cookies

3½ cups vanilla wafers, crushed into fine crumbs

1 cup chopped walnuts

1 cup powdered sugar

⅓ cup peach-flavored bourbon

¼ cup light corn syrup

2 tablespoons unsweetened cocoa powder

6 ounces semisweet chocolate chips

1 tablespoon butter

1. Line cookie sheets with waxed paper.

2. Combine vanilla wafer crumbs, walnuts, powdered sugar, bourbon, corn syrup and cocoa in large bowl; beat by hand until well blended. (Mixture will be very thick and dense.)

3. Shape tablespoonfuls of mixture into balls; place on prepared cookie sheets.

4. Melt chocolate chips and butter in medium saucepan over low heat. Dip balls in chocolate mixture to coat; return to cookie sheets. Refrigerate overnight. Serve chilled.

MAKES ABOUT 6 DOZEN COOKIES

FUN & FROSTY PIES

Pistachio Ice Cream Pie

1 jar (12 ounces) hot fudge dessert topping, divided

1 (6-ounce) chocolate crumb pie crust

2 pints pistachio ice cream, softened

½ cup chopped pistachio nuts

1. Spread half of hot fudge topping over bottom of pie crust; freeze 10 minutes.

2. Spread ice cream evenly over fudge topping; sprinkle with chopped pistachios. Cover and freeze 2 hours or until firm.

3. Let pie stand at room temperature 10 minutes before serving. Warm remaining fudge topping according to package directions; serve with pie.

MAKES 8 SERVINGS

Creamy Peanut Butter Pie

1 cup creamy peanut butter, divided

2 tablespoons corn syrup

1 tablespoon butter

1 (6-ounce) graham cracker pie crust

1 chocolate covered crunchy peanut butter candy bar (2 ounces), crushed, divided

1⅔ cups cold milk

2 packages (4-serving size) instant vanilla pudding and pie filling mix

1 container (8 ounces) whipped topping, thawed, divided

1. Combine ¾ cup peanut butter, corn syrup and butter in medium microwavable bowl. Microwave on HIGH 1 minute; stir until smooth.

2. Spread mixture evenly over bottom of pie crust; sprinkle with 6 tablespoons crushed candy bar.

3. Beat milk and pudding mix in medium bowl with electric mixer at low speed 2 minutes or until thickened. Beat in remaining ¼ cup peanut butter until blended.

4. Remove ½ cup whipped topping from container; set aside. Fold remaining whipped topping into pudding mixture until blended. Spread over peanut butter layer in pie crust. Top with reserved ½ cup whipped topping; sprinkle with remaining crushed candy bar. Refrigerate until ready to serve.

MAKES 8 SERVINGS

Crispy Chocolate Ice Cream Mud Pie

½ cup HERSHEY'S Syrup

⅓ cup HERSHEY'S SPECIAL DARK Chocolate Chips or HERSHEY'S Semi-Sweet Chocolate Chips

2 cups crisp rice cereal

4 cups (1 quart) vanilla ice cream, divided

4 cups (1 quart) chocolate ice cream, divided

Additional HERSHEY'S Syrup

1. Butter 9-inch pie plate.

2. Place ½ cup chocolate syrup and chocolate chips in medium microwave-safe bowl. Microwave at MEDIUM (50%) 45 seconds or until hot; stir until smooth. Reserve ¼ cup chocolate syrup mixture; set aside. Add cereal to remaining chocolate syrup mixture, stirring until well coated; cool slightly.

3. Press cereal mixture, using back of spoon, evenly on bottom and up side of prepared pie plate to form crust. Place in freezer 15 to 20 minutes or until crust is firm. Spread half of vanilla ice cream into crust; spoon reserved ¼ cup chocolate syrup mixture over layer. Spread half of chocolate ice cream over sauce.

4. Top with alternating scoops of vanilla and chocolate ice cream. Cover; return to freezer until serving time. Drizzle with additional chocolate syrup just before serving.

MAKES 8 SERVINGS

Simple Strawberry Cream Pie

4 ounces cream cheese, softened

3 tablespoons sugar

1 (6-ounce) graham cracker pie crust

⅓ cup seedless strawberry fruit spread

3 cups fresh strawberries, hulled and cut into ¼-inch slices

1. Beat cream cheese and sugar in medium bowl until smooth. Spread gently over bottom of pie crust.

2. Whisk fruit spread in small bowl until smooth. Spread 3 tablespoons fruit spread over cream cheese layer.

3. Place strawberries in large bowl. Add remaining fruit spread; toss gently to coat. Arrange berries in crust. Refrigerate 1 hour or until chilled.

MAKES 8 SERVINGS

Frozen Pumpkin Cream Pie

1 cup canned solid-pack pumpkin

⅔ cup KARO® Dark Corn Syrup

½ cup coarsely chopped walnuts

1½ teaspoons SPICE ISLANDS® Pumpkin Pie Spice

2 cups (about 4 ounces) frozen whipped topping, thawed

1 (9-inch) graham cracker crust

Additional whipped topping for garnish (optional)

1. Mix pumpkin, corn syrup, walnuts and pumpkin pie spice in a medium bowl. Fold in whipped topping.

2. Spoon into crust. Cover.

3. Freeze 3 to 4 hours or until firm. Let stand 15 minutes at room temperature before serving. If desired, garnish with additional whipped topping.

MAKES 8 SERVINGS

Prep Time: 10 minutes
Freeze Time: 3 to 4 hours

Simple Strawberry Cream Pie

Creamy Milk Chocolate Pudding Pie

⅔ cup sugar

6 tablespoons cornstarch

2 tablespoons HERSHEY'S Cocoa

½ teaspoon salt

3 cups milk

4 egg yolks

2 tablespoons butter or margarine, softened

1 tablespoon vanilla extract

5 HERSHEY'S Milk Chocolate bars (1.55 ounces each), broken into pieces

1 packaged chocolate crumb crust (6 ounces)

Sweetened whipped cream or whipped topping

Additional HERSHEY'S Milk Chocolate Bar (1.55 ounces), cut into sections along score lines (optional)

1. Stir together sugar, cornstarch, cocoa and salt in 2-quart saucepan. Combine milk and egg yolks in bowl or container with pouring spout. Gradually blend milk mixture into sugar mixture.

2. Cook over medium heat, stirring constantly, until mixture comes to a boil. Boil and stir 1 minute. Remove from heat; stir in butter and vanilla. Add chocolate bar pieces; stir until bars are melted and mixture is well blended. Pour into crumb crust; press plastic wrap onto filling. Cool. Refrigerate several hours or until chilled and firm. Remove plastic wrap. Garnish with whipped cream and chocolate bar sections. Cover; refrigerate leftovers.

MAKES 6 TO 8 SERVINGS

Amaretto Coconut Cream Pie

¼ cup flaked coconut

1 container (8 ounces) frozen whipped topping, thawed, divided

1 container (6 ounces) coconut or vanilla yogurt

¼ cup amaretto liqueur

1 package (4-serving size) coconut instant pudding and pie filling mix

1 (6-ounce) graham cracker pie crust

Fresh strawberries and mint leaves (optional)

1. Spread coconut in medium heavy skillet. Cook over medium heat 1 to 2 minutes until lightly browned, stirring frequently. Remove to small plate to cool.

2. Combine 2 cups whipped topping, yogurt and amaretto in large bowl; stir until blended. Add pudding mix; whisk 2 minutes or until thickened.

3. Spread mixture evenly in pie crust; spread remaining whipped topping over filling. Sprinkle with toasted coconut; garnish with strawberries and mint. Refrigerate until ready to serve.

MAKES 8 SERVINGS

Creamy Cappuccino Frozen Pie

1 package (8 ounces)
    cream cheese, softened

1 can (14 ounces)
    sweetened condensed
    milk

½ cup chocolate syrup

1 tablespoon instant
    coffee granules

1 tablespoon hot water

1½ cups thawed frozen
    whipped topping

1 (6-ounce) chocolate
    crumb pie crust

¼ cup chopped pecans,
    toasted*

Additional chocolate
    syrup

*To toast pecans, spread in
single layer in heavy skillet.
Cook over medium heat 2 to
3 minutes or until nuts are lightly
browned, stirring frequently.

1. Beat cream cheese in large bowl with electric mixer at medium speed 2 to 3 minutes or until fluffy. Add sweetened condensed milk and ½ cup chocolate syrup; beat at low speed until well blended.

2. Dissolve coffee granules in hot water in small bowl. Slowly stir into cream cheese mixture. Fold in whipped topping until blended. Spread mixture in pie crust; sprinkle with pecans. Cover and freeze overnight.

3. Let stand in refrigerator 10 to 15 minutes before serving. Cut into wedges; drizzle with additional syrup.

MAKES 8 SERVINGS

Easy Coconut Banana Cream Pie

1 *prebaked* 9-inch
(4-cup volume)
deep-dish pie shell

1 can (14 ounces)
NESTLÉ® CARNATION®
Sweetened Condensed
Milk

1 cup cold water

1 package (3.4 ounces)
vanilla or banana
cream instant pudding
and pie filling mix

1 cup flaked coconut

1 container (8 ounces)
frozen whipped
topping, thawed,
divided

2 medium bananas, sliced,
dipped in lemon juice

Toasted or tinted flaked
coconut (optional)

COMBINE sweetened condensed milk and water in large bowl. Add pudding mix and coconut; mix well. Fold in *1½ cups* whipped topping.

ARRANGE single layer of bananas on bottom of pie crust. Pour filling into crust. Top with *remaining* whipped topping. Refrigerate for 4 hours or until well set. Top with toasted coconut.

MAKES 8 SERVINGS

Note: To make 2 pies, divide filling between 2 *prebaked* 9-inch (2-cup volume *each*) pie crusts. Top with *remaining* whipped topping.

Prep Time: 20 minutes
Cool Time: 4 hours refrigerating

Crunchy Ice Cream Pie

1 chocolate bar (8 ounces), chopped

2 tablespoons butter

1½ cups crisp rice cereal

½ gallon chocolate chip or fudge ripple ice cream, softened

Hot fudge dessert topping

1. Spray 9-inch pie plate with nonstick cooking spray.

2. Combine chocolate and butter in top of double boiler over simmering water; stir until chocolate is melted and mixture is smooth. Remove from heat. Add cereal; stir until well blended.

3. Spoon mixture into prepared pie plate; press to form crust. Spread ice cream evenly in crust. Cover and freeze until ready to serve.

4. Let stand at room temperature 10 minutes before serving. Drizzle with hot fudge topping.

MAKES 6 SERVINGS

Easy Cherry Cream Pie

1 pint vanilla ice cream, softened

½ (16-ounce) package frozen dark sweet cherries, chopped

1 cup whipping cream

1 tablespoon powdered sugar

⅛ teaspoon almond extract

1 (6-ounce) graham cracker or chocolate crumb pie crust

1. Combine ice cream and cherries in large bowl; stir just until blended.

2. Beat cream, powdered sugar and almond extract in medium bowl with electric mixer at medium-high speed until soft peaks form.

3. Spread ice cream evenly in pie crust. Spread whipped cream over ice cream. Freeze 1 hour or until firm. Let stand at room temperature 10 minutes before serving.

No-Bake Chocolate Cheesecake Pie

1 *prepared* 9-inch (6 ounces) chocolate crumb crust

2 bars (8 ounces) NESTLÉ® TOLL HOUSE® Semi-Sweet Chocolate Baking Bar, melted and cooled

2 packages (8 ounces *each*) cream cheese, softened

¾ cup packed brown sugar

¼ cup granulated sugar

2 tablespoons milk

1 teaspoon vanilla extract

Sweetened whipped cream (optional)

BEAT cream cheese, brown sugar, granulated sugar, milk and vanilla extract in small mixer bowl on high speed for 2 minutes. Add melted chocolate; beat on medium speed for 2 minutes.

SPOON into crust. Refrigerate for 1½ hours or until firm. Top with whipped cream.

MAKES 10 SERVINGS

Easy Cherry Cream Pie

PUDDING PERFECTION

Creamy Brown Rice Pudding

2 cups cooked SUCCESS®, MAHATMA®, CAROLINA® or RICELAND® Whole Grain Brown Rice

1½ cups milk

½ cup maple syrup or honey

1 tablespoon butter

1 teaspoon ground cinnamon, nutmeg or allspice

Combine rice, milk and maple syrup in a medium saucepan. Bring to a boil; reduce heat and simmer 20 minutes, stirring frequently. Remove from heat; stir in butter and cinnamon. Garnish with additional cinnamon, if desired.

MAKES 4 SERVINGS

Rocky Road Pudding

5 tablespoons
   unsweetened
   cocoa powder

¼ cup granulated sugar

3 tablespoons cornstarch

⅛ teaspoon salt

2½ cups milk

2 egg yolks, beaten

2 teaspoons vanilla

¼ cup sugar

1 cup mini marshmallows

¼ cup chopped walnuts,
   toasted*

*To toast walnuts, spread in
single layer in heavy skillet.
Cook over medium heat 3 to
4 minutes or until nuts are
lightly browned and fragrant,
stirring frequently.*

1. Combine cocoa, granulated sugar, cornstarch and salt in small saucepan; stir until well blended. Stir in milk until smooth.

2. Cook over medium-high heat about 10 minutes or until mixture thickens and begins to boil, stirring constantly.

3. Whisk ½ cup hot milk mixture into beaten egg yolks in small bowl. Pour mixture back into saucepan; cook over medium heat about 10 minutes or until mixture reaches 160°F, whisking constantly. Remove from heat; stir in vanilla.

4. Place plastic wrap on surface of pudding. Refrigerate about 20 minutes or until slightly cooled. Stir in sugar. Spoon pudding into six dessert dishes; top with marshmallows and walnuts.

MAKES 6 SERVINGS

Citrus Tapioca Pudding

2 navel oranges

2½ cups milk

⅓ cup sugar

3 tablespoons quick-cooking tapioca

1 egg, beaten

½ teaspoon almond extract

Ground cinnamon or nutmeg

Additional orange slices (optional)

1. Grate peel of 1 orange into medium saucepan. Stir in milk, sugar, tapioca and egg; let stand 5 minutes.

2. Bring to a boil over medium heat, stirring constantly. Remove from heat; stir in almond extract. Let stand 20 minutes. Stir pudding and let cool to room temperature. Cover and refrigerate at least 2 hours.

3. Peel and dice oranges. Stir pudding; gently fold in oranges. Spoon into dessert dishes. Sprinkle with cinnamon; garnish with additional orange slices.

MAKES 8 SERVINGS

Chocolate Pudding Parfaits

2 ounces semisweet
   chocolate, chopped

2 ounces white chocolate,
   chopped

½ cup sugar

2 tablespoons all-purpose
   flour

1 tablespoon cornstarch

2¼ cups milk

2 egg yolks, beaten

2 teaspoons vanilla

1. Place semisweet chocolate and white chocolate in separate heatproof bowls.

2. Whisk sugar, flour and cornstarch in small saucepan. Gradually whisk in milk. Cook over medium heat until mixture comes to a boil, stirring constantly. Boil 2 minutes, stirring constantly.

3. Remove saucepan from heat. Whisk small amount of hot milk mixture into egg yolks in small bowl. Pour egg mixture back into saucepan; cook and stir over low heat until thickened. Remove from heat; stir in vanilla.

4. Spoon half of egg yolk mixture over each chocolate; stir until chocolates are completely melted.

5. Alternate layers of puddings in parfait glasses. Cover and refrigerate until chilled.

MAKES 3 TO 4 SERVINGS

Classic Minute Rice Pudding

3 cups milk

1 cup MINUTE® White Rice, uncooked

¼ cup sugar

¼ cup raisins

¼ teaspoon salt

2 eggs

1 teaspoon vanilla

Combine milk, rice, sugar, raisins and salt in medium saucepan. Bring to a boil, stirring constantly. Reduce heat to medium-low; simmer 6 minutes, stirring occasionally.

Beat eggs and vanilla lightly in small bowl. Stir small amount of hot mixture into eggs. Stirring constantly, slowly pour egg mixture back into hot mixture.

Cook over low heat 1 minute, stirring constantly, until thickened. DO NOT BOIL. Remove from heat. Let stand 30 minutes.

Serve warm. Store any remaining pudding in refrigerator.

MAKES 4 SERVINGS

Tip: Create flavorful new varieties of rice puddings by trying different types of dried fruits instead of raisins, such as dried cherries, chopped dried apricots, chopped dried pineapple or dried sweetened cranberries.

White Chocolate Pudding with Crunchy Toffee Topping

¼ cup sugar

¼ cup cornstarch

¼ teaspoon salt

2 cups milk

¾ cup whipping cream

6 squares (1 ounce each) white chocolate, chopped

2 teaspoons vanilla

Crunchy Toffee Topping (recipe follows)

1. Combine sugar, cornstarch and salt in medium saucepan; stir until well blended. Slowly whisk in milk and cream, stirring constantly. Bring to a boil over medium heat, stirring constantly. Reduce heat to low; cook and stir 2 to 3 minutes or until thickened.

2. Remove saucepan from heat; stir in chocolate and vanilla until chocolate is completely melted. Spoon into six dessert dishes; cover with plastic wrap. Refrigerate 1 hour or up to 2 days.

3. Prepare Crunchy Toffee Topping. Just before serving, sprinkle topping over pudding.

MAKES 6 SERVINGS

Crunchy Toffee Topping:
Spray 10-inch square sheet of foil with nonstick cooking spray. Combine ½ cup sugar and ½ cup light corn syrup in medium microwavable bowl; microwave on HIGH 4 minutes. (Mixture will be light brown in color.) Stir in 1 cup sliced almonds and 2 teaspoons butter; microwave 2 minutes. Stir in ½ teaspoon baking soda and ½ teaspoon vanilla. (Mixture will foam.) Spread mixture in thin layer on prepared foil; cool completely. Break into pieces.

Peaches and Cinnamon Rice Pudding

1 cup water

⅓ cup uncooked rice (not converted)

1 tablespoon butter

⅛ teaspoon salt

1 can (16 ounces) sliced peaches in juice, undrained

½ cup milk, divided

2 teaspoons cornstarch

½ teaspoon ground cinnamon

¼ cup plus 1 tablespoon peach fruit spread, divided

½ cup whipping cream

Additional peach fruit spread (optional)

1. Combine water, rice, butter and salt in medium saucepan; bring to a boil over high heat. Reduce heat to low; cover and simmer 25 minutes or until rice is tender. Remove from heat.

2. Drain canned peaches, reserving ½ cup juice. Set peaches aside. Stir reserved juice and ¼ cup milk into rice.

3. Whisk cornstarch and cinnamon in small bowl. Gradually whisk in remaining ¼ cup milk until smooth. Add to rice mixture; bring to a boil over medium-high heat, stirring constantly. Reduce heat to low; simmer 2 minutes or until thickened, stirring frequently. Remove from heat; stir in ¼ cup fruit spread. Cool to room temperature, stirring occasionally.

4. Chop peaches; stir into pudding. Spoon pudding into four dessert dishes.

5. Beat cream and remaining 1 tablespoon fruit spread in medium bowl with electric mixer at medium-high speed until soft peaks form. Spoon over pudding. Drizzle with additional fruit spread, if desired.

MAKES 4 SERVINGS

Tutti Frutti Pudding Cones

2 cups milk

⅓ cup sugar

¼ cup quick-cooking
    tapioca

1 egg, beaten

1 teaspoon vanilla

½ to ¾ cup yogurt (cherry,
    raspberry, strawberry,
    lime or lemon)

4 to 6 small flat-bottomed
    ice cream cones

1. Combine milk, sugar, tapioca and egg in medium saucepan; whisk until well blended. Let stand 5 minutes.

2. Bring to a boil over medium heat, stirring constantly. Remove from heat; stir in vanilla. Cover and let cool 20 minutes. (Pudding can be refrigerated up to 2 days after cooling.)

3. For each cone, combine 2 tablespoons pudding and 2 tablespoons yogurt in small bowl; stir until well blended. Spoon into ice cream cone; serve immediately.

MAKES 4 TO 6 SERVINGS

Variation: Stir small pieces of fresh fruit into the pudding mixture for additional fruit flavor.

Chocolate Chip Pudding

2 cups milk

⅓ cup CREAM OF WHEAT®
Hot Cereal (Instant,
1-minute, 2½-minute or
10-minute cook time),
uncooked

1 tablespoon butter

1 tablespoon unsweetened
cocoa powder

½ teaspoon salt

¼ cup semisweet chocolate
chips

1 cup marshmallow crème

Whipped cream
(optional)

Additional unsweetened
cocoa powder
(optional)

Semisweet mini chocolate
chips (optional)

1. Heat milk in saucepan over medium heat until it just begins to bubble. Add Cream of Wheat, butter, 1 tablespoon cocoa and salt. Cook and stir 5 minutes or until mixture thickens.

2. Add ¼ cup chocolate chips. Cook and stir until chocolate melts. Remove from heat. Stir in marshmallow crème, a little at a time. Serve warm. Garnish with whipped cream, cocoa and mini chocolate chips, if desired.

MAKES 4 SERVINGS

Tip: For a delicious taste twist, substitute butterscotch chips or white chocolate chips for the semisweet chocolate chips.

Prep Time: 15 minutes
Start to Finish Time: 15 minutes

FROZEN TREATS

Frozen Caramel Chocolate Dessert Squares

4 chocolate graham
crackers

1 package (4-serving size)
vanilla instant pudding
and pie filling mix

1 cup milk

4 ounces cream cheese,
softened

1 container (8 ounces)
frozen whipped
topping, thawed

¼ cup mini chocolate chips

4 tablespoons dulce de
leche (see Note)

1. Layer graham crackers
in bottom of 8-inch square
baking dish, breaking
crackers to fit. Whisk
pudding mix and milk in
small bowl until blended.

2. Beat cream cheese in large bowl
with electric mixer at medium speed until
smooth and fluffy. Add pudding mixture;
beat until blended. Whisk in whipped
topping until blended. Stir in chocolate
chips. Pour mixture over graham crackers
in baking dish.

3. Pour dulce de leche into small
microwavable bowl. Microwave on
HIGH about 45 seconds or just until
softened. Swirl dulce de leche into cream
cheese mixture with spoon. Cover with
plastic wrap; freeze overnight.

MAKES 9 SERVINGS

Note: Dulce de leche is caramelized
milk popular in Latin cooking. It is
available in cans and jars at most large
supermarkets in the Hispanic food aisle
or in the evaporated milk section. If
dulce de leche is not available, substitute
caramel ice cream topping.

Frozen Chocolate Banana Pops

3 bananas, peeled

6 ice cream sticks or wooden skewers

½ cup semisweet chocolate chips

1½ teaspoons vegetable oil

¼ cup sprinkles, coconut, chopped peanuts or crushed cookies (optional)

1. Line baking sheet with waxed paper or foil. Cut each banana in half. Insert ice cream stick halfway into each banana. Place on prepared baking sheet; freeze 1 hour.

2. Combine chocolate chips and oil in small saucepan; stir over low heat until melted and smooth. Place toppings on individual plates, if using.

3. Remove bananas from freezer. Spoon chocolate over each banana while holding banana over saucepan. Roll in toppings to coat. Return to baking sheet; freeze about 1 hour or until chocolate and toppings are set. Store in airtight container or resealable freezer food storage bag.

MAKES 6 SERVINGS

Note: If desired, bananas can be cut into 1-inch pieces, frozen, then dipped in chocolate for individual bites.

Mocha Semifreddo Terrine

1½ teaspoons espresso powder

⅓ cup boiling water

2½ cups (4 ounces) amaretti cookies (about 35 cookies)

1 tablespoon unsweetened cocoa powder

3 tablespoons butter, melted

8 egg yolks

¾ cup plus 2 tablespoons sugar, divided

1 cup whipping cream

1. Dissolve espresso powder in boiling water; set aside to cool.

2. Line 9×5-inch loaf pan with plastic wrap. Combine cookies and cocoa in food processor; process until cookies are finely ground. Add butter; process until well blended. Press mixture into bottom of prepared pan. Place in freezer while preparing custard.

3. Whisk egg yolks and ¾ cup sugar in top of double boiler or in medium metal bowl. Stir in espresso mixture. Place over simmering water; cook 4 to 5 minutes or until thickened, whisking constantly. Remove from heat; place bowl in pan of ice water. Whisk mixture 1 minute. Let stand in ice water 5 minutes or until cooled to room temperature, whisking occasionally.

4. Beat cream and remaining 2 tablespoons sugar in large bowl with electric mixer at high speed until stiff peaks form. Gently fold whipped cream into cooled custard. Spread mixture over crust in loaf pan. Cover tightly with plastic wrap; freeze until firm, at least 8 hours or up to 24 hours before serving.

5. Invert terrine onto serving plate; remove plastic wrap. Cut into slices. Serve on chilled plates.

MAKES 8 TO 12 SERVINGS

Double Berry Pops

2 cups plain Greek yogurt, divided

1 cup fresh blueberries

3 tablespoons sugar, divided

6 (5-ounce) paper or plastic cups or pop molds

1 cup sliced fresh strawberries

6 pop sticks

1. Combine 1 cup yogurt, blueberries and 1½ tablespoons sugar in blender or food processor; blend until smooth.

2. Pour mixture into cups. Freeze 2 hours.

3. Combine strawberries, remaining 1 cup yogurt and 1½ tablespoons sugar in blender or food processor; blend until smooth.

4. Pour mixture over blueberry layer in cups. Cover top of each cup with small piece of foil. Freeze 2 hours.

5. Insert sticks through center of foil. Freeze 4 hours or until firm.

6. To serve, remove foil and peel away paper cups or gently twist frozen pops out of plastic cups.

MAKES 6 POPS

Coffee Toffee
Ice Cream Sandwiches

1 cup coffee ice cream

¼ cup milk chocolate
toffee bits

8 vanilla pizzelles

1. Let ice cream stand at room temperature 10 minutes or until slightly softened. Place toffee bits in shallow dish.

2. Carefully spread ¼ cup ice cream over 1 pizzelle. Top with second pizzelle; press together lightly. Roll edge in toffee bits. Repeat with remaining ingredients.

3. Wrap each sandwich in plastic wrap; freeze overnight or until firm.

MAKES 4 SANDWICHES

Tip: You can substitute 1 toffee candy bar, crushed, for the toffee baking bits.

Cantaloupe Sorbet

6 cups cubed peeled
cantaloupe

⅓ cup light corn syrup

3 tablespoons lime juice

1. Place cantaloupe in food processor; process until puréed. Add corn syrup and lime juice; process until blended. Pour into medium bowl; refrigerate until cold.

2. Freeze cantaloupe mixture in ice cream maker according to manufacturer's directions.

MAKES 4 CUPS

Coffee Toffee
Ice Cream Sandwiches

Cinnamon-Honey Pops

1¼ cups plain Greek yogurt

½ cup honey

¼ cup milk

1 tablespoon sugar

½ teaspoon ground cinnamon

½ teaspoon vanilla

Pop molds or paper or plastic cups

Pop sticks

1. Combine yogurt, honey, milk, sugar, cinnamon and vanilla in blender or food processor; blend until smooth.

2. Pour mixture into molds. Cover top of each mold with small piece of foil. Freeze 2 hours.*

3. Insert sticks through center of foil. Freeze 4 hours or until firm.

4. To remove pops from molds, remove foil and place bottoms of pops under warm running water until loosened. Press firmly on bottoms to release. (Do not twist or pull sticks.)

*If using pop molds with lids, skip step 3 and freeze until firm.

MAKES 6 POPS

Dutch Country Dirt

Chocolate wafer cookies

2 to 3 tablespoons HERSHEY'S Syrup

2 scoops (about ½ cup each) chocolate ice cream, softened

½ cup HERSHEY'S MINI KISSESBRAND Milk Chocolates

1 tablespoon HERSHEY'S Cocoa or HERSHEY'S SPECIAL DARK Cocoa

1 tablespoon powdered sugar

1. Crush 1 to 2 cookies; place on bottom of ice cream dish. Cover cookies with chocolate syrup.

2. Combine 1 scoop chocolate ice cream with chocolate pieces; place on top of cookies and syrup. Top with second scoop chocolate ice cream.

3. Stir together cocoa and powdered sugar; sprinkle over ice cream. Garnish as desired.

MAKES 1 SERVING

Paradise Pops

1 cup milk

¾ cup frozen or fresh pineapple chunks

¾ cup frozen or fresh chopped mango

¼ cup unsweetened coconut milk

1 tablespoon honey

Pop molds or paper or plastic cups

Pop sticks

1. Combine milk, pineapple, mango, coconut milk and honey in blender or food processor; blend until smooth.

2. Pour mixture into molds. Cover top of each mold with small piece of foil. Freeze 1 hour. Insert sticks through center of foil. Freeze 6 hours or until firm.

3. To remove pops from molds, remove foil and place bottoms of pops under warm running water until loosened. Press firmly on bottoms to release. (Do not twist or pull sticks.)

MAKES 4 POPS

Dutch Country Dirt

Strawberry-Banana Granité

2 ripe medium bananas, peeled and sliced (about 2 cups)

2 cups frozen strawberries (do not thaw)

¼ cup strawberry pourable fruit*

Fresh mint leaves (optional)

Or substitute 3 tablespoons strawberry fruit spread combined with 1 tablespoon warm water.

1. Place banana slices in resealable freezer food storage bag; freeze until firm.

2. Combine bananas and strawberries in food processor or blender; let stand 10 minutes to soften slightly.

3. Add pourable fruit to food processor. Remove plunger from top of food processor to allow air to be incorporated. Process until smooth, scraping down sides of bowl frequently. Garnish with mint, if desired. Serve immediately.

MAKES 5 SERVINGS

Note: Granité can be transferred to airtight container and frozen up to 1 month. Let stand at room temperature 10 minutes to soften slightly before serving.

Candy Bar Pops

1 pint (2 cups) vanilla ice cream

1 bar (about 2 ounces) chocolate-covered peanut, caramel and nougat candy, chopped

½ cup chopped honey-roasted peanuts

¼ cup caramel ice cream topping

Pop sticks

3 ounces semisweet chocolate, melted

1. Scoop ice cream into chilled large metal bowl. Cut in chopped candy, peanuts and caramel topping with pastry blender or two knives; fold and cut again. Repeat until mixture is evenly incorporated, working quickly. Cover and freeze 1 hour.

2. Line baking sheet with plastic wrap. Scoop 10 balls of ice cream mixture onto baking sheet. Freeze 1 hour.

3. Reshape ice cream into balls, if necessary. Insert sticks; freeze 1 hour or until firm.

4. Drizzle melted chocolate over pops. Freeze 30 minutes to 1 hour or until firm.

MAKES 10 POPS

Speedy Pineapple-Lime Sorbet

1 ripe pineapple, cut into cubes (about 4 cups)

⅓ cup frozen limeade concentrate

1 to 2 tablespoons lime juice

1 teaspoon grated lime peel

1. Arrange pineapple in single layer on large baking sheet; freeze at least 1 hour or until very firm.*

2. Combine frozen pineapple, limeade concentrate, lime juice and lime peel in food processor or blender; process until smooth and fluffy. If mixture doesn't become smooth and fluffy, let stand 30 minutes to soften slightly; repeat processing. Serve immediately.

*Pineapple can be frozen up to 1 month in resealable freezer food storage bags.

MAKES 8 SERVINGS

Note: This dessert is best served immediately, but it can be made ahead, stored in the freezer and then softened several minutes before being served.

COOL & CREAMY

Cherry Parfait Crunch

¾ **pound dark or light sweet cherries**

½ **cup unsweetened apple juice**

¼ **teaspoon ground cinnamon**

Dash ground nutmeg

1 **teaspoon cornstarch**

1 **tablespoon water**

⅓ **cup natural wheat and barley cereal**

2 **tablespoons chopped toasted almonds**

2 **cups vanilla yogurt**

1. Remove stems and pits from cherries; cut into halves (about 2¼ cups).

2. Combine cherries, apple juice, cinnamon and nutmeg in small saucepan; cook and stir over medium heat 5 minutes or until cherries begin to soften.

3. Whisk cornstarch and water in small bowl until smooth; stir into saucepan. Cook and stir over high heat until mixture boils and thickens slightly. Let cool 10 minutes; cover and refrigerate until chilled.

4. Combine cereal and almonds in small bowl. Layer half of cherry mixture, half of yogurt and half of cereal mixture in four parfait or wine glasses; repeat layers.

MAKES 4 SERVINGS

Summer Strawberry Orange Cups

2 cups fresh strawberries, hulled, divided

1 package (¼ ounce) unflavored gelatin

2 tablespoons cold water

2 tablespoons boiling water

1½ cups milk

½ cup frozen orange juice concentrate

1 teaspoon vanilla

Fresh mint leaves (optional)

1. Cut 1 cup strawberries into thin slices; place in bottom of six 8-ounce dessert dishes or custard cups.

2. Combine gelatin and cold water in small bowl; let stand 5 minutes. Add boiling water to softened gelatin; stir until completely dissolved.

3. Combine milk, orange juice concentrate and vanilla in medium bowl; stir until well blended. Let stand at room temperature 20 minutes. Stir in gelatin mixture until well blended. Pour evenly over sliced strawberries in dessert dishes. Refrigerate 2 hours or until completely set.

4. Slice remaining 1 cup strawberries; top each dessert with strawberry slices and mint, if desired.

MAKES 6 SERVINGS

Pumpkin Mousse Parfaits

2 ounces cream cheese,
softened

1 can (15 ounces)
solid-pack pumpkin

¾ cup milk

1 package (4-serving size)
vanilla instant pudding
and pie filling mix

1 teaspoon ground
cinnamon

½ teaspoon ground ginger

⅛ teaspoon ground cloves

3 cups frozen whipped
topping, thawed,
divided

4 gingersnap cookies,
crushed

1. Beat cream cheese in medium bowl with electric mixer at medium speed until smooth. Add pumpkin, milk, pudding mix, cinnamon, ginger and cloves; beat 1 minute or until smooth. Fold in 1½ cups whipped topping.

2. Spoon ¼ cup mousse into each of eight 6-ounce dessert glasses. Spoon 2 tablespoons whipped topping over each dessert; top with ¼ cup mousse. Cover and refrigerate 1 hour.

3. Just before serving, top each parfait with remaining whipped topping and gingersnap crumbs.

MAKES 8 SERVINGS

Easy Fruit Parfaits

1 cup boiling water

1 package (4-serving size)
gelatin, any red flavor

1 cup cold water

Frozen nondairy
whipped topping,
thawed

1 can (15.25 ounces)
DOLE® Tropical Fruit,
drained

1. Stir boiling water into gelatin in medium bowl 2 minutes until completely dissolved. Stir in cold water. Pour gelatin into 4 tall dessert or parfait glasses, filling about half full.

2. Refrigerate 4 hours or until firm. To serve, layer with whipped topping and tropical fruit.

MAKES 4 SERVINGS

Pumpkin Mousse Parfaits

Deep Dark Mousse

¼ cup sugar

1 teaspoon unflavored gelatin

½ cup milk

1 cup HERSHEY'S SPECIAL DARK Chocolate Chips

2 teaspoons vanilla extract

1 cup (½ pint) cold whipping cream

Sweetened whipped cream (optional)

1. Stir together sugar and gelatin in small saucepan; stir in milk. Let stand 2 minutes to soften gelatin. Cook over medium heat, stirring constantly, until mixture just begins to boil.

2. Remove from heat. Immediately add chocolate chips; stir until melted. Stir in vanilla; cool to room temperature.

3. Beat whipping cream in medium bowl with electric mixer on high speed until stiff peaks form. Add half of chocolate mixture and gently fold until nearly combined. Add remaining chocolate mixture and fold just until blended. Spoon into serving dish or individual dishes. Refrigerate. Garnish with sweetened whipped cream, if desired, just before serving.

MAKES 4 TO 6 SERVINGS

Raspberry Chantilly Parfait

1 container (6 ounces) vanilla yogurt

¼ cup sifted powdered sugar

1 package (10 ounces) frozen raspberries in light syrup, thawed

4 cups frozen whipped topping, thawed

1⅓ cups crushed oatmeal cookies or granola cereal

1⅓ cups fresh blueberries

1. Spread yogurt to ½-inch thickness on several layers of paper towels; place two layers of paper towels over yogurt. Let stand 15 minutes. Scrape yogurt from paper towels into large bowl using rubber spatula. Stir in sugar.

2. Place raspberries in food processor or blender; process until smooth. Pour through fine-meshed sieve into bowl; press raspberries with back of spoon against sides of sieve to squeeze out liquid. Discard seeds. Stir into yogurt until blended. Fold in whipped topping.

3. Spoon half of yogurt mixture into four parfait glasses; sprinkle with half of crushed cookies and blueberries. Repeat layers. Serve immediately or cover and refrigerate up to 2 hours.

MAKES 4 SERVINGS

Tip: To use whipped cream instead of whipped topping, beat 2 cups chilled whipping cream with ¼ cup powdered sugar in large bowl with electric mixer at medium-high speed until stiff peaks form. Fold into yogurt mixture and proceed as directed.

Strawberry Mousse

1 package (4-serving size) strawberry gelatin

½ cup boiling water

2 cups fresh sliced strawberries, divided

½ cup cream cheese, softened

½ cup cold water

¼ teaspoon almond extract

1 cup frozen whipped topping, thawed, plus additional for garnish

1. Place gelatin in small bowl. Pour boiling water over gelatin; stir until completely dissolved.

2. Pour gelatin mixture into blender. Add 1 cup sliced strawberries, cream cheese, cold water and almond extract; blend 1 minute or until completely smooth.

3. Pour mixture into medium bowl. Add 1 cup whipped topping; whisk until well blended (make sure gelatin mixture does not settle to bottom of bowl).

4. Spoon mousse into six dessert dishes. Refrigerate at least 2 hours or until set. Top with remaining sliced strawberries and additional whipped topping, if desired.

MAKES 6 SERVINGS

Chocolate Cookie Parfaits

1 package (4-serving size) chocolate instant pudding and pie filling mix

2 cups milk

8 tablespoons frozen whipped topping, thawed

4 chocolate sandwich cookies, finely crushed

4 teaspoons multi-colored sprinkles

1. Prepare pudding according to package directions using 2 cups milk.

2. Spoon half of pudding into four parfait glasses. Spread 1 tablespoon whipped topping over pudding in each glass; sprinkle with half of crushed cookies. Layer remaining pudding over cookies. Top with remaining whipped topping, cookies and sprinkles.

MAKES 4 SERVINGS

Blackberry Panna Cotta

3 cups frozen blackberries, thawed

2 cups whipping cream

1 cup buttermilk

¾ cup sugar

3 tablespoons water

1 package (¼ ounce) unflavored gelatin

1. Place blackberries in food processor or blender; process until smooth.

2. Combine cream, buttermilk and sugar in

medium saucepan over medium heat. Add blackberry purée; bring to a simmer over low heat.

3. Pour water into small saucepan. Sprinkle with gelatin; heat over low heat, swirling pan until gelatin is dissolved. Add to blackberry mixture; stir until blended.

4. Strain mixture through fine mesh sieve or strainer, pressing down with rubber spatula. Pour evenly into six 8-ounce ramekins or custard dishes. Refrigerate 6 hours or until set. Invert and unmold onto serving plates.

MAKES 6 SERVINGS

Chocolate Cookie Parfaits

Mandarin Mousse Mold

1½ cups boiling water

1 package (8-serving size) **or** 2 packages (4-serving size) orange or mango flavor gelatin

1 cup cold water

1 can (11 **or** 15 ounces) DOLE® Mandarin Oranges, drained

1 tub (8 ounces) frozen nondairy whipped topping, thawed, divided

1. Stir boiling water into gelatin in large bowl 2 minutes until completely dissolved.

2. Stir in cold water. Place mandarin oranges into 6-cup mold; spoon 2 cups gelatin mixture into mold over oranges. Refrigerate about 30 minutes or until set, but not firm (should stick to finger and mound).

3. Meanwhile, refrigerate remaining gelatin mixture about 30 minutes or until slightly thickened (consistency of unbeaten egg whites). Stir in 2 cups of the whipped topping with wire whisk until smooth. Pour over gelatin layer in mold.

4. Refrigerate 4 hours or until firm. Unmold. Garnish with remaining whipped topping. Store leftover gelatin mold in refrigerator.

Unmolding: Dip mold in warm water for about 15 seconds. Gently pull gelatin from around edges with moist fingers. Place moistened serving plate on top of mold. Invert mold and plate; holding mold and plate together, shake slightly to loosen. Gently remove mold and center gelatin on plate.

MAKES 12 SERVINGS

Mango White Chocolate Mousse

1 cup whipping cream

1¼ cups mango or apricot nectar, divided

½ tablespoon unflavored gelatin

4 ounces white chocolate

1. Beat cream in large bowl with electric mixer at medium-high speed until stiff peaks form. Cover and refrigerate.

2. Place ¼ cup nectar in small microwavable bowl. Sprinkle with gelatin; let stand 5 minutes. Microwave on HIGH 45 seconds; stir until gelatin is dissolved.

3. Bring ½ cup water to a simmer in medium saucepan. Combine white chocolate and remaining 1 cup mango nectar in medium bowl. Place bowl over simmering water; whisk until chocolate is melted. Add gelatin mixture; whisk until well blended. Remove bowl from saucepan; place on wire rack 30 minutes or until cool.

4. Fold whipped cream into white chocolate mixture. Spoon into six dessert dishes. Cover with plastic wrap; refrigerate 4 hours or until set.

MAKES 6 SERVINGS

Blue Pom Dessert

1 cup frozen sweetened raspberries, thawed

4 envelopes (1 ounce) unflavored gelatin

3 cups pomegranate juice

1 cup fresh blueberries

1. Place raspberries in medium bowl; sprinkle with gelatin. Bring juice to a boil in medium saucepan over medium-high heat. Pour boiling juice over raspberries; stir until gelatin is dissolved.

2. Divide blueberries among four to six 8-ounce molds. Strain raspberry mixture through sieve or fine mesh strainer into measuring cup; pour evenly over blueberries.

3. Refrigerate about 3 hours or until set. Invert onto individual dessert plates.

MAKES 4 TO 6 SERVINGS

Milk Chocolate Pots de Crème

2 cups (11.5-ounce package) HERSHEY'S Milk Chocolate Chips

½ cup light cream

½ teaspoon vanilla extract

Sweetened whipped cream (optional)

1. Place chocolate chips and light in medium microwave-safe bowl. Microwave at MEDIUM (50%) 1 minute; stir. If necessary, microwave at MEDIUM an additional 15 seconds at a time, stirring after each heating, just until chocolate is melted and smooth when stirred. Stir in vanilla.

2. Pour into demitasse cups or very small dessert dishes. Cover; refrigerate until firm. Serve cold with sweetened whipped cream, if desired.

MAKES 6 TO 8 SERVINGS

Blue Pom Dessert

Berry-Quinoa Parfaits

⅔ cup uncooked quinoa

2 cups plus 2 tablespoons milk, divided

⅛ teaspoon salt

¼ cup sugar

1 egg

1½ teaspoons vanilla

2 cups sliced fresh strawberries

¼ cup vanilla yogurt

Ground cinnamon (optional)

1. Place quinoa in fine-mesh strainer; rinse well under cold running water. Combine quinoa, 2 cups milk and salt in medium saucepan; bring to a simmer over medium heat. Reduce heat to medium-low; simmer, uncovered, 20 to 25 minutes or until quinoa is tender, stirring frequently.

2. Whisk remaining 2 tablespoons milk, sugar, egg and vanilla in medium bowl until well blended. Gradually whisk ½ cup hot quinoa mixture into egg mixture, then whisk mixture back into saucepan. Cook over medium heat 3 to 5 minutes or until bubbly and thickened, stirring constantly. Remove from heat; let cool 30 minutes.

3. Layer quinoa mixture and strawberries in six parfait dishes. Top with yogurt and sprinkle with cinnamon, if desired.

MAKES 6 SERVINGS

DECADENT DESSERTS

No-Bake Chocolate Cake Roll

1 package (4-serving size) vanilla instant pudding and pie filling mix

3 tablespoons HERSHEY'S Cocoa, divided

1 cup milk

1 container (8 ounces) frozen non-dairy whipped topping, thawed and divided

1 package (9 ounces) crisp chocolate wafers

HERSHEY'S HUGSBRAND Candies and HERSHEY'S KISSESBRAND Milk Chocolates

1. Combine pudding mix and 2 tablespoons cocoa in small bowl. Add milk; beat on low speed of electric mixer until smooth and thickened. Fold in 1 cup whipped topping, blending well.

2. Spread about 1 tablespoon pudding mixture onto top of each chocolate wafer; put wafers together in stacks of 4 or 5. On foil, stand wafers on edge to make one long roll. Wrap tightly; refrigerate 5 to 6 hours.

3. Sift remaining 1 tablespoon cocoa over remaining 2½ cups whipped topping; blend well. Unwrap roll; place on serving tray. Spread whipped topping mixture over entire roll. Remove wrappers from candies; place on roll to garnish. To serve, slice diagonally at 45-degree angle. Cover; refrigerate leftover dessert.

MAKES ABOUT 12 SERVINGS

Easy Citrus Berry Shortcake

2 individual sponge cakes

2 tablespoons orange juice

½ cup lemon chiffon-flavored yogurt

½ cup thawed frozen nondairy whipped topping

1⅓ cups sliced fresh strawberries or raspberries

Fresh mint leaves (optional)

1. Place sponge cakes on individual serving plates. Drizzle with orange juice.

2. Combine yogurt and whipped topping in small bowl; stir gently until blended.

3. Spoon one quarter of mixture onto each cake. Top with strawberries and remaining yogurt mixture; garnish with mint leaves.

MAKES 2 SERVINGS

Strawberry Cheesecake Dessert

2 cups graham cracker crumbs

⅓ cup butter, melted

¼ cup granulated sugar

2 packages (8 ounces each) cream cheese, softened

1 cup powdered sugar

2 containers (6 ounces each) lemon yogurt

3 pints fresh strawberries, hulled and sliced

1 container (12 ounces) frozen whipped topping, thawed

1. Combine graham cracker crumbs, butter and granulated sugar in medium bowl; mix well. Press into bottom of 13×9-inch baking dish.

2. Beat cream cheese and powdered sugar in medium bowl with electric mixer at medium speed 1 minute or until creamy. Add yogurt; beat until well blended. Pour mixture over crust.

3. Arrange strawberries over cream cheese mixture. Spread whipped topping over strawberries. Refrigerate at least 4 hours or overnight.

MAKES 9 TO 12 SERVINGS

Easy Citrus Berry Shortcake

Pear Crêpes

2 large ripe pears, seeded and thinly sliced

⅓ cup packed brown sugar

¼ cup water

¼ teaspoon ground cinnamon

⅛ teaspoon Chinese five-spice powder*

¼ teaspoon salt

2 teaspoons lemon juice

4 (10-inch) prepared crêpes**

½ cup mascarpone cheese or whipped ricotta cheese

2 teaspoons granulated sugar

¼ cup chopped glazed walnuts (optional)

*Chinese five-spice powder consists of cinnamon, cloves, fennel seed, star anise and Szechuan peppercorns. It can be found in most supermarkets and at Asian markets.

**Ready-to-use crêpes are available in the supermarket produce section.

1. Combine pears, brown sugar, water, cinnamon, five-spice powder and salt in medium saucepan; cook over medium-high heat 10 minutes or until pears are soft and liquid evaporates, stirring occasionally. Stir in lemon juice; set aside to cool slightly.

2. To assemble, warm each crêpe in microwave oven according to package directions. Spread generous ⅓ cup filling on one quarter of each crêpe. Fold in half, then into quarters; place on serving plate.

3. Combine mascarpone cheese and granulated sugar in small bowl; stir until blended. Spoon 2 tablespoons mixture over each crêpe. Sprinkle with glazed walnuts, if desired.

MAKES 4 SERVINGS

Chocolate Chili and Orange Fondue

2 bars (4 ounces each) 60 to 70% bittersweet chocolate, coarsely chopped

2 tablespoons butter, softened

1½ cups whipping cream

½ cup frozen orange juice concentrate, thawed but not diluted

1 teaspoon vanilla

½ teaspoon ancho or chipotle chili powder

1. Place chopped chocolate and butter in medium bowl.

2. Bring cream to a boil in small saucepan over medium heat; pour over chocolate. Add orange juice concentrate, vanilla and chili powder; stir until chocolate is melted and mixture is smooth.

3. Serve immediately in individual bowls or fondue pot.

MAKES 6 SERVINGS

Tip: Serve fondue alongside an assortment of dippers such as strawberries, orange segments, apple slices, pear slices, pineapple chunks, banana slices, cookies, marshmallows, pound cake cubes or large pretzel rods.

Cinnamon Tacos with Fruit Salsa

1 cup sliced fresh
strawberries

1 cup cubed fresh
pineapple

1 cup cubed peeled kiwi

½ teaspoon ORTEGA®
Diced Jalapeños

4 tablespoons plus
1 teaspoon granulated
sugar, divided

1 tablespoon ground
cinnamon

6 (8-inch) ORTEGA® Flour
Soft Tortillas

Nonstick cooking spray

Stir together strawberries, pineapple, kiwi, jalapeños and 4 teaspoons sugar (adjust to taste, if desired) in large bowl; set aside.

Combine remaining 3 tablespoons sugar and cinnamon in small bowl; set aside.

Coat tortillas lightly on both sides with nonstick cooking spray. Heat each tortilla in nonstick skillet over medium heat until slightly puffed and golden brown. Remove from heat; immediately dust both sides with cinnamon-sugar mixture. Shake excess cinnamon-sugar back into bowl. Repeat cooking and dusting process until all tortillas are warmed.

Fold tortillas in half and fill with fruit mixture. Serve immediately.

MAKES 6 SERVINGS

Prep Time: 20 minutes
Start to Finish Time: 30 minutes

Peanut Butter Fondue

Selection of fruits and
other fondue dippers

3⅓ cups (two 10-ounce
packages) REESE'S
Peanut Butter Chips

1½ cups light cream

1. Prepare ahead of time a selection of fresh fruit chunks for dipping: apples, bananas, pears, peaches, cherries, pineapple and/or oranges (brush fresh fruit with lemon juice to prevent browning). Cover; refrigerate until ready to serve. (Dried apples and apricots, marshmallows and bite-size pieces of pound cake can also be used for dipping.)

2. Place peanut butter chips and cream in medium microwave-safe bowl. Microwave at MEDIUM (50%) 1½ minutes; stir. If necessary, microwave at MEDIUM an additional 30 seconds at a time, stirring after each heating, until chips are melted and mixture is smooth when stirred.

3. Pour into fondue pot; keep warm over low heat. Dip chunks of fruit into warm sauce with forks. Keep leftover sauce covered and refrigerated.

MAKES ABOUT 3 CUPS FONDUE

Note: Recipe may be halved using 1 package (10 ounces) REESE'S Peanut Butter Chips and ¾ cup light cream.

Blackberry Lemon Cheesecake Trifle

1 package (8 ounces) cream cheese, softened

⅓ cup lemon juice

1 can (14 ounces) sweetened condensed milk

2 cups frozen nondairy whipped topping, thawed

1 package (10¾ ounces) frozen pound cake, thawed

¼ cup frozen lemonade concentrate

¼ cup water

1 jar (10 ounces) seedless blackberry jam, melted

6 cups fresh or thawed frozen blackberries

1. Beat cream cheese and lemon juice in medium bowl with electric mixer at medium speed until smooth and creamy. Add sweetened condensed milk; beat until blended. Fold in whipped topping.

2. Cut pound cake into ¼-inch-thick slices. Arrange half of cake slices in bottom of trifle dish or large glass bowl.

3. Combine lemonade concentrate and water in small bowl. Brush half of lemonade mixture over cake; let stand 5 minutes. Brush half of jam over cake. Spoon half of cream cheese mixture over jam; top with half of berries. Repeat layers with remaining ingredients. Cover with plastic wrap; refrigerate overnight.

MAKES 10 TO 12 SERVINGS

Peanutty Crispy Dessert Cups

⅓ cup creamy peanut
butter

2 tablespoons butter

3 cups large marshmallows
(5 ounces)

3 cups chocolate-flavored
crisp rice cereal

Ice cream or frozen
yogurt

Chocolate sauce, colored
candies and sprinkles,
chopped peanuts
and/or maraschino
cherries

1. Heat peanut butter and butter in large saucepan over low heat until melted and smooth. Add marshmallows; cook until melted, stirring constantly. Remove saucepan from heat; stir in cereal until well blended and cooled slightly.

2. Scoop mixture evenly into 12 standard (2½-inch) nonstick muffin cups; press into bottoms and up sides of cups.

3. Refrigerate 5 to 10 minutes or until set. Remove cups from pan; fill with ice cream and sprinkle with desired toppings.

MAKES 12 SERVINGS

Black Forest Tiramisù

½ cup hot water

2 teaspoons instant espresso powder or instant coffee granules

8 ounces mascarpone cheese, at room temperature

1 package (4-serving size) chocolate instant pudding and pie filling mix

2 cups whipping cream

1 cup milk

24 ladyfingers

1 can (16 ounces) cherry pie filling

¼ cup kirsch or cherry liqueur

1. Combine hot water and espresso powder in small bowl; stir until espresso is dissolved.

2. Beat mascarpone in large bowl with electric mixer at medium speed about 15 seconds or until fluffy. Add pudding mix; beat until blended. Slowly add cream; beat at low speed 2 minutes or until fluffy. Add milk; beat 1 minute or until creamy.

3. Arrange 12 ladyfingers in 9-inch square baking dish. Brush half of espresso mixture over ladyfingers with pastry brush. Spread half of mascarpone mixture evenly over ladyfingers. Repeat layers.

4. Combine cherry pie filling and kirsch in medium bowl; spread over top of tiramisù. Cover and refrigerate overnight.

MAKES 9 SERVINGS

Cannoli Napoleons

1 container (15 ounces) whole milk ricotta cheese

¾ cup mascarpone cheese

⅔ cup powdered sugar

1½ teaspoons grated orange peel

1 teaspoon vanilla

12 vanilla pizzelles

⅓ cup grated semisweet chocolate

Sweetened whipped cream

6 tablespoons chopped toasted pistachio nuts*

*To toast pistachios, cook and stir nuts in small skillet over medium heat 6 to 8 minutes or until lightly browned.

1. Combine ricotta cheese, mascarpone cheese, powdered sugar, orange peel and vanilla in large bowl; stir until well blended. Cover and refrigerate 30 minutes or up to 24 hours.

2. For each napoleon, place 1 pizzelle on dessert plate. Spread ¼ cup ricotta mixture over pizzelle; sprinkle with generous 1 teaspoon chocolate. Repeat layers. Top with whipped cream and sprinkle with 1 tablespoon pistachios. Serve immediately.

MAKES 6 SERVINGS

Acknowledgments

*The publisher would like to thank the companies and organizations
listed below for the use of their recipes in this publication.*

ACH Food Companies, Inc.

Cream of Wheat® Cereal, A Division of B&G Foods North America, Inc.

Dole Food Company, Inc.

The Hershey Company

Nestlé USA

Ortega®, A Division of B&G Foods North America, Inc.

Riviana Foods Inc.

Metric Conversion Chart

VOLUME MEASUREMENTS (dry)

1/8 teaspoon = 0.5 mL
1/4 teaspoon = 1 mL
1/2 teaspoon = 2 mL
3/4 teaspoon = 4 mL
1 teaspoon = 5 mL
1 tablespoon = 15 mL
2 tablespoons = 30 mL
1/4 cup = 60 mL
1/3 cup = 75 mL
1/2 cup = 125 mL
2/3 cup = 150 mL
3/4 cup = 175 mL
1 cup = 250 mL
2 cups = 1 pint = 500 mL
3 cups = 750 mL
4 cups = 1 quart = 1 L

VOLUME MEASUREMENTS (fluid)

1 fluid ounce (2 tablespoons) = 30 mL
4 fluid ounces (1/2 cup) = 125 mL
8 fluid ounces (1 cup) = 250 mL
12 fluid ounces (1 1/2 cups) = 375 mL
16 fluid ounces (2 cups) = 500 mL

WEIGHTS (mass)

1/2 ounce = 15 g
1 ounce = 30 g
3 ounces = 90 g
4 ounces = 120 g
8 ounces = 225 g
10 ounces = 285 g
12 ounces = 360 g
16 ounces = 1 pound = 450 g

DIMENSIONS

1/16 inch = 2 mm
1/8 inch = 3 mm
1/4 inch = 6 mm
1/2 inch = 1.5 cm
3/4 inch = 2 cm
1 inch = 2.5 cm

OVEN TEMPERATURES

250°F = 120°C
275°F = 140°C
300°F = 150°C
325°F = 160°C
350°F = 180°C
375°F = 190°C
400°F = 200°C
425°F = 220°C
450°F = 230°C

BAKING PAN SIZES

Utensil	Size in Inches/Quarts	Metric Volume	Size in Centimeters
Baking or Cake Pan (square or rectangular)	8×8×2	2 L	20×20×5
	9×9×2	2.5 L	23×23×5
	12×8×2	3 L	30×20×5
	13×9×2	3.5 L	33×23×5
Loaf Pan	8×4×3	1.5 L	20×10×7
	9×5×3	2 L	23×13×7
Round Layer Cake Pan	8×1½	1.2 L	20×4
	9×1½	1.5 L	23×4
Pie Plate	8×1¼	750 mL	20×3
	9×1¼	1 L	23×3
Baking Dish or Casserole	1 quart	1 L	—
	1½ quart	1.5 L	—
	2 quart	2 L	—